Best Easy Day Hikes Series

Best Easy Day Hikes
Dallas/Fort Worth

Ka

FALCONGUIDES

GUILFORD, CONNECTICUT
HELENA, MONTANA

AN IMPRINT OF GLOBE PEQUOT PRESS

FALCONGUIDES®

Copyright © 2010 by Morris Book Publishing, LLC

Project editor: Jessica Haberman
Maps: Off Route Inc. © Morris Book Publishing, LLC

TOPO! Explorer software and SuperQuad source maps courtesy of
National Geographic Maps. For information about TOPO! Explorer,
TOPO!, and Nat Geo Maps products, go to www.topo.com or www
.natgeomaps.com.

Library of Congress Cataloging-in-Publication Data
Hopper, Kathryn.
  Best easy day hikes, Dallas/Fort Worth / Kathryn Hopper.
      p. cm.
  ISBN 978-0-7627-5293-5
  1. Hiking–Texas–Dallas–Guidebooks. 2. Hiking–Texas–Fort Worth–
Guidebooks. 3. Dallas (Tex.)–Guidebooks. 4. Fort Worth (Tex.)–
Guidebooks. I. Title.
  GV199.42.T492D354 2010
  917.64'2812–dc22
                                                     2009026709
Printed in the United States of America
10 9 8 7 6 5 4 3 2 1

917.6428
H0

Contents

The Hikes

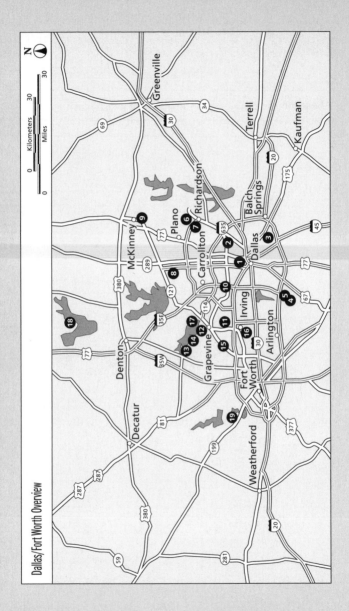

Dallas/Fort Worth Overview

Acknowledgments

Thanks to my hiking partners, including Stuart, James, Henry, Will, and Andrew Tonkinson. For advice on birds and other wildlife, thanks to the Dallas Chapter of the National Audubon Association, Bob Jones Nature Center, the Fort Worth Nature Center, and Heard Nature Museum and Wildlife Sanctuary. And special thanks to Bud Kennedy.

Introduction

North Texas is not a traditional hiking mecca, but the region's 6.1 million-plus residents can actually find a wide variety of trails, from urban walks through trendy neighborhoods to rural retreats by tranquil lakes—all within an hour's drive. This pocket guide contains nineteen easy day hikes in North Texas ranging in length from 0.75 mile to just over 6.0 miles. These hikes cover a variety of ecosystems, from the wide-open spaces of the blackland prairie to the wooded glens of the Cross Timbers. Area elevations generally range from 450 to 600 feet. A few places, like Cedar Ridge Preserve southwest of Dallas, have similar geological roots to the Texas Hill Country in and around Austin, with rocky limestone ledges and scrubby cedar forests.

Both Dallas and Fort Worth are nestled on the banks of the Trinity River, and while the river has been little more than a drainage ditch in some areas, cities are investing millions of dollars in projects to enhance their waterfronts and protect the region's vibrant floodplains—home to the nation's largest urban hardwood forest. The region's numerous lakes, all man-made and created to supply the area's ever-growing water demands, also provide sites for gorgeous hiking trails.

Although the Metroplex is more famous for its massive malls and sports arenas, the region is actually home to several top-notch nature preserves that offer a much-needed escape from suburban sprawl. Indeed it's possible to find secluded trails nestled along bubbling streams only a few hundred yards from bustling highways. *Best Easy Day Hikes Dallas/Fort Worth* showcases the best of this region's recreational riches.

Weather

An advantage North Texas offers over northern climes is year-round hiking weather. Sure summer days can be scorching, with temperatures routinely topping the 100-degree mark, but humidity typically drops and night-time temperatures fall to the upper 70s, making for pleasant evening hikes. Winters here are generally mild, with daytime highs often topping 70 degrees, making for some of the best hiking months of the year. Another plus for fall hiking: Trails are largely deserted on weekends as folks take in another fall tradition—football. In winter, sudden cold fronts can move in, dipping temperatures below freezing, but snow is rare and fleeting. Winter also offers less-crowded trails and the ability to spot bird and squirrel nests in bare trees. Winter is the mating season for some species here, including coyotes, which are most commonly spotted at sunrise and sunset.

Spring brings rainy weather and fast-moving fronts that can trigger straight-line winds, tornadoes, and hail. Much of the Dallas/Fort Worth area is equipped with outdoor warning sirens that go off when dangerous tornados and large hail are approaching. If you find yourself on the trail when a storm pops up, head for cover if at all possible, and stay away from lone trees, lakes, and open areas.

The old North Texas saying "If you don't like the weather, just wait five minutes and it'll change" is a reminder to be prepared for any and all types of weather when heading out for a hike. Temperatures can drop 50 degrees or more in less than an hour, so check the weather report, and dress in layers when appropriate.

Wilderness Restrictions and Regulations

Trails in this guide are located in city parks, state parks, wildlife refuges, and lands managed by the U.S. Army Corps of Engineers. Most trails located in city parks do not require special use permits or charge use fees. Texas state parks charge an admission fee, or you can purchase an annual pass that's good for unlimited entry in the state's more than ninety parks and covers everyone in the car or up to five people in your party if you enter via bike or foot. Passes are sold at most parks or can be ordered by calling (512) 389-8900.

Some trails are located in areas maintained by nonprofit groups such as the National Audubon Society and ask for donations in lieu of entrance fees. See trail descriptions for more information.

Safety and Preparation

Generally speaking, the most common wildlife encounters in North Texas are with squirrels, birds, and the occasional armadillo. Bobcats and coyotes also make their home here, but they present more danger to small pets than to people. North Texas is home to several varieties of poisonous snakes, including copperheads and rattlesnakes, and warning signs dot several trails, advising hikers to watch their step and not stray off the marked path. It's also a good idea to hike in closed-toed shoes, not only to avoid stepping on a snake while you're wearing sandals but also to avoid the wrath of fire ants and thorny plants, from cacti to horse nettle.

In tornado season, check the forecast before you head out and avoid hiking if there's a thunderstorm or a tornado watch. After a heavy rain, the region's heavy clay soils become muddy quagmires and bubbling streams turn into raging rivers, so consider trail conditions before heading out. Some dirt trails may be closed a day or two after a heavy rain. It's smart to pack a light rain jacket in case a sudden shower comes up, and you're likely to need a jacket fall through spring, when balmy days can quickly turn chilly after sundown.

While some trails have water fountains, many don't, so pack one or two water bottles even for short hikes—more if you're hiking with children and dogs. It's also smart to wear sunscreen and a hat even on cloudy days. Long pants can save your legs from brambles and branches that grow over many trails. Mosquito repellent is recommended spring through fall, particularly when you're hiking around sunrise and sunset, when the pests are most active.

Careful use of maps and this guide should keep you from getting lost, but if you do lose your way, stop and retrace your route until you can reorient yourself. Most of the hikes in this book are well marked and frequently traveled, but it's wise to carry a GPS unit and bring a cell phone with you just in case of emergency. If possible, hike with a friend or join a local hiking group to combine fellowship and fun while hitting the trail.

Hiking Organizations

Cross Timbers Lone Star Chapter of the Sierra Club
1900 Highland Park Circle
Denton, TX 76205-6932
(940) 891-4984
http://texas.sierraclub.org/crosstimbers/index.html

Greater Fort Worth Sierra Club
P.O. Box 1874
Burleson, TX 76097
(817) 588-1167
www.lonestar.sierraclub.org/fortworth/

Dallas Sierra Club
P.O. Box 800365
Dallas, TX 75380
(214) 369-5543
www.texas.sierraclub.org/dallas

Dallas Trekkers
P.O. Box 743813
Dallas, TX 75374-3813
(214) 732-3419
www.dallastrekkers.org

Zero Impact

Many trails in the Dallas/Fort Worth region are heavily
used year-round. We, as trail users and advocates, must be
especially vigilant to make sure our passage leaves no lasting
mark. Here are some basic guidelines for preserving trails in
the region:

- Pack out all your own trash, including biodegradable
  items like orange peels. You might also pack out gar-
  bage left by less-considerate hikers.

- Don't approach or feed any wild creatures—the ground
  squirrel eyeing your snack food is best able to survive if
  it remains self-reliant.

- Don't pick wildflowers or gather rocks, antlers, feathers, and other treasures along the trail. Removing these items will only take away from the next hiker's experience.

- Avoid damaging trailside soils and plants by remaining on the established route. This is also a good rule of thumb for avoiding poison oak and stinging nettle, common regional trailside irritants.

- Don't cut switchbacks, which can promote erosion.

- Be courteous by not making loud noises while hiking.

- Many of these trails are multiuse, which means you'll share them with other hikers, trail runners, cyclists, mountain bikers, and equestrians. Familiarize yourself with the proper trail etiquette, yielding the trail when appropriate.

- Use restrooms or outhouses at trailheads or along the trail.

How to Use This Guide

This guide is designed to be simple and easy to use. Each hike is described with a map and summary information that delivers the trail's vital statistics, including distance and type of trail (loop, lollipop, or out and back), approximate hiking time, difficulty, trail surface, best season to hike the trail, other trail users, canine compatibility, fees and permits, park schedule, sources for additional maps, and trail contacts. If there's something else you need to know about the trail, we'll tell you that too. Directions to the trailhead are also provided, along with a general description of what you'll see along the way. A detailed route finder (Miles and Directions) sets forth mileages between significant landmarks along the trail.

Hike Selection

This guide describes trails that are accessible to every hiker, whether visiting from out of town or someone lucky enough to live in Dallas/Fort Worth. The hikes are no longer than 7.0 miles round-trip, and some are considerably shorter. They range in difficulty from flat excursions perfect for a family outing to more challenging treks up ridges and ravines. While these trails are among the best, keep in mind that nearby trails, often in the same park or preserve, may offer options better suited to your needs. I've sought to space hikes throughout the Dallas/Fort Worth area, so wherever your starting point, you'll find a great easy day hike nearby.

Difficulty Ratings

These are all easy hikes, but easy is a relative term. To aid in the selection of a hike that suits particular needs and abilities, each is rated easy, moderate, or more challenging. Bear in mind that even challenging routes can be made easy by hiking within your limits and taking rests when you need them.

Easy hikes are generally short and flat, taking no longer than an hour to complete.

Moderate hikes involve increased distance and relatively mild changes in elevation, and will take one to two hours to complete.

More challenging hikes feature some steep stretches, greater distances, and generally take longer than two hours to complete.

These are completely subjective ratings—what you think is easy is entirely dependent on your level of fitness and the adequacy of your gear (primarily shoes). If you are hiking with a group, you should select a hike with a rating that's appropriate for the least fit and prepared in your party.

Approximate hiking times are based on the assumption that on flat ground, most walkers average 2 miles per hour. Adjust that rate by the steepness of the terrain and your level of fitness (subtract time if you're an aerobic animal and add time if you're hiking with kids), and you have a ballpark hiking duration. Be sure to add more time if you plan to picnic or take part in other activities like bird watching or photography.

Trail Finder

Best Hikes for River and Creek Lovers

- 3   Trinity River Audubon Center
- 6   Breckenridge Park
- 10   L. B. Houston Nature Trail
- 16   River Legacy Park Trail

Best Hikes for Lake Lovers

- 12   Lake Grapevine Horseshoe Trail
- 13   Walnut Grove Trail
- 17   North Shore Trail
- 18   Ray Roberts Lake State Park: Johnson Branch Trail

Best Hikes for Children

- 3   Trinity River Audubon Center
- 9   Heard Wildlife Sanctuary: Wood Duck Trail
- 14   Bob Jones Nature Center Trail
- 15   Colleyville Nature Center Trail

Best Hikes for Dogs

- 1   Katy Trail
- 11   Little Bear Creek Trail
- 12   Lake Grapevine Horseshoe Trail
- 16   River Legacy Park Trail

Best Hikes for Great Views

- 2   White Rock Lake Trail
- 5   Cedar Ridge Preserve: Cattail Pond Trail
- 8   Arbor Hills Loop

Best Hikes for Nature Lovers

Map Legend

══30══	Interstate Highway
══377══	U.S. Highway
══18══	State Highway
═════	Local Roads
- - - - - - -	Unpaved Roads
▬▬▬▬▬▬	Featured Route
- - - - - - - - -	Trail
┼─┼─┼─┼─┼	Railroad
～～～～	River/Creek
⸺⸺	Marsh/Swamp
⬭	Lake/Pond
‖‖‖‖‖‖	Boardwalk
⊃⊂	Bridge
▦	Bench
🅿	Parking
🛆	Picnic Area
■	Point of Interest/Structure
🚻	Restroom
○	Town
❶❶	Trailhead
🏞	Viewpoint/Overlook
⋙	Waterfall

1 Katy Trail

The former railroad right-of-way has gone from neighborhood eyesore to the place to see and be seen in uptown Dallas. It's the closest thing North Texas hiking has to a singles bar, as the city's buff and beautiful sweat out romance. Some couples have even married on the trail. But don't feel put off if you're not in the market. The trail welcomes all ages, as long as you don't try to wander into the adjacent private homes and apartment complexes.

Distance: 5.0 miles out and back

Approximate hiking time: 1.5 to 2 hours

Difficulty: Easy

Trail surface: Concrete with side trail made out of pedestrian-friendly soft surface

Best season: Mar through June; Oct through Dec

Other trail users: Runners, cyclists, in-line skaters, dog walkers

Canine compatibility: Leashed dogs permitted

Fees and permits: No fees or permits required

Schedule: Park open daily 5:00 a.m. to midnight

Maps: TOPO! Texas CD; Friends of the Katy Trail map

Trail contacts: The trail is operated by the Dallas Parks and Recreation Department but is largely maintained and improved by the very active Friends of the Katy Trail; (214) 303-1180; www.katytraildallas.org.

Special considerations: The biggest bummer about the Katy Trail is the lack of restrooms. There are a few portable toilets in Reverchon Park but nothing along the trail. And don't think you can slip into the woods—both sides of the trail are densely populated, and you could end up on someone's back patio. At Knox Street you can stop for a drink at one of the bistros or grab a latte at a coffee shop and use the facilities, otherwise—sweat it out.

Finding the trailhead: From downtown Dallas, take Woodhall Rogers Freeway north to the Pearl Street exit. Go north on Pearl to Maple Avenue and follow Maple Avenue to entrance of Reverchon Park at 3535 Maple Ave. From the park's parking lot, walk toward Turtle Creek. Exit at the stone bridge and veer right on the trail, passing playgrounds on the right. The trail winds up a hill by a stone pavilion to the Katy Trail. GPS: N32 48.078' / W96 48.625'

The Hike

Located on the old railbed of the Missouri–Kansas–Texas, or MKT, Railroad (nicknamed Katy for short), this trail was born in 1997 to preserve the narrow greenbelt and create an urban path traveling north from downtown Dallas to posh Highland Park and beyond. The 12-foot-wide concrete path is supplemented by an 8-foot-wide soft-surface trail for pedestrians in many but not all areas.

One of the easiest places to access the trail is from Reverchon Park, where the Friends of the Katy Trail, a volunteer organization of more than 1,200 enthusiasts, raised more than $1.5 million to construct an elaborate stone entrance. The trail actually begins 0.5 mile to the south. If time permits, you can take a right at the trailhead and hike the short distance to enjoy a view of downtown Dallas and the American Airlines Center.

From the Reverchon entrance, simply veer left and start heading north, walking between upscale apartment and office buildings on the right and leafy Turtle Creek on the left. The trail is a straight shot, with no street crossings up to Knox Street, the border of Highland Park. Mileage markers are embedded in the trail every 0.25 mile, beginning at the American Airlines Center. From the south the markers go up to 3.5 miles and then return to zero.

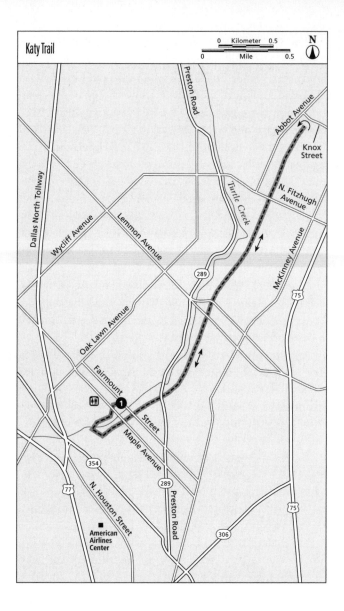

Katy Trail

0 Kilometer 0.5
0 Mile 0.5

N

Preston Road
Abbot Avenue
Knox Street
N. Fitzhugh Avenue
Turtle Creek
McKinney Avenue
75
289
Dallas North Tollway
Wycliff Avenue
Lemmon Avenue
Oak Lawn Avenue
Fairmount Street
Maple Avenue
Preston Road
354
77
N. Houston Street
American Airlines Center
289
306
75

The trail is very well populated—crowded even on weekends and after work—making it feel relatively safe during those times. Dallas Police officers patrol the trail on bikes, and Friends of the Katy Trail can be spotted making the rounds on a golf cart. In 2008 the city added "911" markers every one-eighth mile along a 3.5-mile stretch of the trail. At the bottom of these markers, labeled KT-100 through KT-125, are numbers indicating the GPS coordinates to help determine your location in an emergency—the Katy Trail doesn't have an official address.

The trail continues to grow, spreading north from Highland Park to Southern Methodist University, and should eventually connect to the Mockingbird DART Station and a trail heading east to White Rock Lake. The trail is great for people watching—both fellow hikers and cyclists on the trail and residents perched on patios overlooking the trail. (Some upscale developments now use the trail as an amenity to boost adjacent property prices.)

As you cross over Cedar Springs Road, take a look to your left toward Turtle Creek at the pinkish building styled like a sixteenth-century Italian Renaissance villa. That's the luxurious Mansion on Turtle Creek hotel, where rock stars and other celebrities routinely hang their hats—and perhaps hit the trail.

Pass over Hall Street and Lemmon Avenue. Turn around at Knox Street, but be sure to go all the way to the intersection. Otherwise you might miss Christopher Janney's soundscape titled *Parking in Color,* which creates what he calls "urban musical instruments" for passers-by.

Miles and Directions

0.0   Start at Reverchon Park. Head uphill through the stone plaza to the trail entrance.

0.75 Cross the bridge over Cedar Springs Road.

2.5   Turn around at Knox Street and head south, retracing your route to trailhead.

5.0   Arrive back at the trailhead.

2 White Rock Lake Trail

Before air-conditioning, White Rock Lake was where Dallasites went to cool off and teens cruised along winding Lawther Drive. But when city officials banned swimming and disconnected the scenic waterside byway in four places, the park slowly went into decline. Now runners, cyclists, and hikers have rediscovered the scenic loop, thanks to continual improvements that are adding new luster to this city jewel.

Distance: 4.5 miles out and back

Approximate hiking time: 1.5 to 2 hours

Difficulty: Moderate; relatively flat terrain, but winds off the lake can add to the workout

Trail surface: Paved

Best season: Feb through May

Other trail users: Very popular with cyclists

Canine compatibility: Leashed dogs permitted

Fees and permits: No fees or permits required

Schedule: Park open daily 5:00 a.m. to 11:00 p.m.

Maps: TOPO! Texas CD; maps available online at www.white rocklake.org

Trail contacts: Dallas Parks and Recreation; (214) 670-4100; www.dallasparks.org

For the Love of the Lake, a nonprofit organization that supports the lake; www.whiterock lake.org

Special considerations: Coyotes have been spotted at dawn and dusk by the lake, particularly when mating season peaks around Valentine's Day.

While the city has beefed up security around the lake, it's still advisable to hike with a partner, particularly at dusk or when you walk through the more remote, forested parts of the trail.

Note that this trail is under construction until 2010. Call ahead for information about trail closings during that time.

Finding the trailhead: Take the Mockingbird Lane exit off US 75, traveling east. Exiting at West Lawther Drive, follow the winding road south, around the lake. Lawther intersects White Rock Road in a tight corner; look for a railroad trestle overhead. Veer right onto White Rock Road; pass a pumping station on the right and continue to a large parking lot next to a fishing dock. The trail begins from this lot, located at 2920 White Rock Lake Rd. GPS: N32 49.384' / W96 43.803'

The Hike

Created in 1911 to be the main water source for the growing city of Dallas, White Rock Lake no longer quenches thirst but has become the primary recreational outlet for the city's west side. The lake has an interesting history, having once housed 200 or so Civilian Conservation Corps (CCC) workers in the 1930s at a campsite on Winfrey Point. Their handiwork is evident in many of the lake's art deco buildings and monuments.

The lake is bounded by the quiet Lakewood neighborhood to the east and Garland Road on the west side, where you'll also find the Dallas Arboretum and the Bathhouse Cultural Center, a local theater hot spot. The lake also is home to one of the city's most famous ghosts—the Lady of the Lake, an apparition of a young woman that's occasionally spotted along the roads and paths circling the lake. For more lake lore, check out the White Rock Lake Museum, located in the cultural center at 521 East Lawther Dr. (214-670-8749).

The lake is in the middle of major refurbishing, including a new 911 system to help rescue workers better locate those in need. Trail improvements include a promenade and viewing area by the lake's famous spillway, damaged by

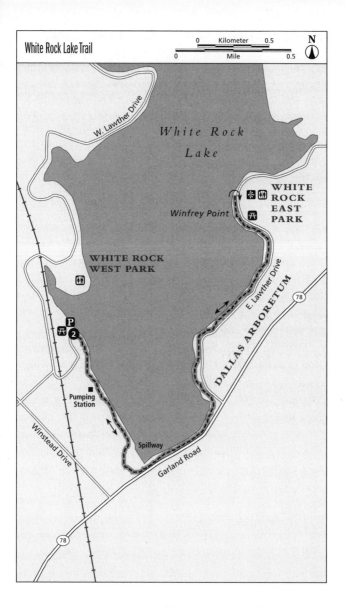

White Rock Lake Trail

0   Kilometer   0.5

0   Mile   0.5

N

White Rock Lake

W. Lawther Drive

Winfrey Point

WHITE ROCK EAST PARK

WHITE ROCK WEST PARK

P

2

E. Lawther Drive

DALLAS ARBORETUM

78

Pumping Station

Winstead Drive

Spillway

Garland Road

78

heavy rains in 2006. The $17 million project is expected to be completed in 2010. Until then, expect occasional detours in and around this part of the lake's trail.

The trailhead is located in the parking lot, just north of the pumping station. Pass the station, built in 1911 but no longer a working facility. If the trail is under construction here, you'll have to backtrack to the last trail junction and veer left into a former railroad bed through the forest. If you are not detoured, the trail continues to the spillway before veering right to go through the woods toward Winstead Road. There you'll come to parking area where the trail veers left toward Garland Road and then heads northwest, running alongside the busy road.

At East Lawther Drive veer left and hike alongside the drive, passing the Dallas Arboretum on the right. A chain-link fence separates the trail from the gorgeous gardens, but you can still steal a few glimpses of the flowers and Rancho Encinal, the Spanish Colonial–style home built by pioneering geophysicist Everette Lee DeGolyer and his wife, Nell, in 1940. Bequeathed to Southern Methodist University, the estate eventually became the property of the city of Dallas and now is a venue for parties and other events at the arboretum.

The trail continues to Winfrey Point, where you can catch a view of downtown Dallas before heading back to the trailhead. If you want to extend your hike, continue approximately 6.0 miles to loop around the lake.

Miles and Directions

0.0 Start by the fishing pier and veer left out of the parking lot.

0.1 Take the paved trail to the left and pass a pumping station.

0.8 Bear left as the trail follows Winstead Drive and then turn left as the trail runs alongside Garland Road.

1.3 Veer left as trail follows East Lawther Drive, passing Dallas Arboretum on the right.

2.25 Come to Winfrey Point. Take in the view from the shore, or head up to the highest point for a view of the Dallas skyline before retracing your steps.

4.5 Arrive back at the trailhead.

3 Trinity River Audubon Center

Opened in 2008, this Leadership in Energy and Environmental Design (LEED)–certified education center and the surrounding nature preserve are popular with schoolchildren and birders drawn by informative programs and abundant wildlife. This trail takes in an expansive view of the Trinity River then heads through a prairie and adjacent woodland before circling back to the education center.

Distance: 1.0 mile out and back

Approximate hiking time: 30 minutes

Difficulty: Easy

Trail surface: Boardwalk and packed dirt

Best season: Late Mar through May; Oct and Nov

Other trail users: Very popular with birders, school field trips, and scout groups

Canine compatibility: No dogs permitted

Fees and permits: Admission fee; no charge for children 2 and under

Schedule: Center open Tues through Sat 9:00 a.m. to 4:00 p.m.; Sun 10:00 a.m. to 5:00 p.m.; closed Mon

Maps: TOPO! Texas CD; maps available at education center

Trail contacts: Trinity River Audubon Center; (214) 398-TRAC (8722); www.tx.audubon.org

Special considerations: The third Thursday of each month is Free Thursday, with free admission and extended operating hours (9:00 a.m. to 9:00 p.m.).

Collecting plants is prohibited, as is attempting to touch, feed, or help any wildlife encountered in the preserve.

Finding the trailhead: Take I-45 south from downtown Dallas to Loop 12. Go east on Loop 12 for approximately 2 miles. Look for the entrance sign on the right side of the highway at 6500 South Loop 12. GPS: N32 38.283' / W96 57.549'

The Hike

A large informative map detailing the various trails in the preserve is adjacent to the entrance of the education center. For this trail, combine the 0.3-mile Trinity River Trail with the 0.65-mile Forest Trail. You can easily add on the inter-connecting 0.4-mile Overlook Trail, hiking up a small hill to take in a blufftop view from the preserve's tallest point, and the 0.9-mile Wetland Trail and 0.5 mile Prairie Trail, which together wind through several ponds frequented by a variety of ducks and egrets.

Enter the education center, where you'll pass an infor-mation desk and classrooms plus a large open lecture room, and exit through the glass doors in the rear. The trailhead begins on the boardwalk over the appropriately named Trailhead Pond, the junction for several trails. Veer right onto the Trinity River Trail, heading away from the pond and into the open prairie. At 0.15 mile the trail splits. Bear left into the forest and wind under the dense overstory of ancient oaks to a rustic wooden fence, where you can take in the view of a bend in the Trinity River. Turn around and head back to the spot where the trail splits. This time go straight onto the Forest Trail. You'll pass three large ponds in an open prairie where birders like to look for birds resting on tree limbs above the grasses.

The trail continues toward a wooded area and loops around two smaller ponds. Snakes sometimes rest on and alongside the trails, so keep an eye on the trail even as you look up to spot birds. Don't wander off the well-marked trail—poison ivy grows rampantly in these woods. The Forest Trail loops around back to the junction with the Trinity River Trail, so simply wind your way back to Trailhead Pond.

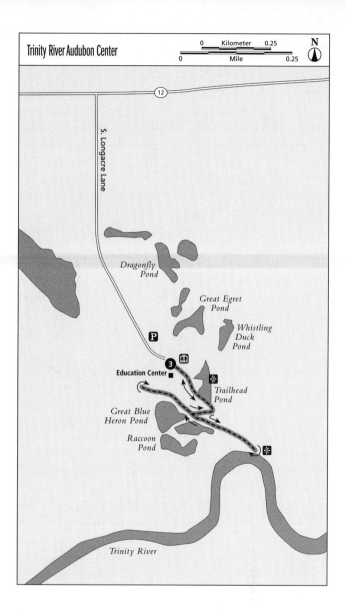

0   Kilometer   0.25
0   Mile   0.25
N

S. Longacre Lane

12

Dragonfly
Pond

Great Egret
Pond

Whistling
Duck
Pond

P

3

Education Center

Trailhead
Pond

Great Blue
Heron Pond

Raccoon
Pond

Trinity River

If time permits, head over to the lookout platform across from the center and check out some of the other trails. Otherwise, head back through the center and exit to the parking lot. On the south side of the building, a large bank of solar cells helps power the preserve's utilities and educational markers explain various ways to minimize human impact on the earth's resources.

Miles and Directions

0.0 Start at the boardwalk over Trailhead Pond. Bear right at the junction onto the Trinity River Trail, heading toward the prairie.

0.15 Veer left when the trail splits, and head into the forest.

0.3 The trail dead-ends at Trinity River. Turn around and head back toward the education center.

0.5 At the trail junction go straight onto the Forest Trail, passing three ponds on the left.

0.7 Enter the forest and loop around counterclockwise back to the three ponds.

0.8 Bear left at the trail junction and head back to Trailhead Pond and the education center.

1.0 Arrive back at the trailhead.

4 Cedar Hill State Park: Talala Trail

Located only 10 miles southwest of downtown Dallas, this trail feels worlds away as it winds through the westernmost vestiges of blackland prairie on the way to Joe Pool Lake. The nearby Penn Farm Agricultural History Center provides a hands-on history lesson.

Distance: 1.8-mile lollipop
Approximate hiking time: 1 hour
Difficulty: Moderate; can be difficult to follow
Trail surface: Packed dirt and grass
Best season: Feb through May
Other trail users: None
Canine compatibility: Leashed dogs permitted
Fees and permits: Admission fee; no charge for children 12 and under
Schedule: Park open daily 8:00 a.m. to 10:00 p.m. (gates locked)

Maps: TOPO! Texas CD; park maps showing trails available at entrance gate
Trail contacts: Texas Parks and Wildlife; (800) 792-1112; www .tpwd.state.tx.us
Special considerations: Much of the trail is through open fields, so wear a hat and sunscreen.
In addition: Texas Parks and Recreation periodically offers guided hikes and child-friendly talks about the park's animal residents. For more information call (972) 291-5940.

Finding the trailhead: From US 67 take exit 1382 and go 2.5 miles north. The park is on the left. From I-20 take exit FM1382 and drive 4 miles south. The park is on the right. From the park entrance turn left onto South Spine Road and look for the Talala Trail parking lot, 0.5 mile on the left. The trailhead is adjacent to the parking lot, by the information sign. GPS: N32 36.987' / W96 58.879'

The Hike

The Cedar Hill area offers a unique landscape in North Texas as the blackland prairie pushes into Dallas's own mini mountain range. The Cedar Mountains are a mix of Austin Chalk limestone and Eagle Ford shale, which after millions of years of erosion, created a tight series of craggy hills and valleys covered in upland forests of cedars and scrubby oaks and elms. For hikers that means lots of up-and-down trails—a departure from the typically smooth or gradually rising and falling trails in the region. The park is located on the western edge of the blackland prairie, which once covered a great swath of the midsection of America and into Canada but has been plowed over so that only a tiny fraction remains. The dense black soil turns to thick muck after a heavy rain. When it dries, it creates mounds, which some early settlers called "hog wallow."

In 1854 John Anderson Penn settled in the rugged Cedar Mountains, and the land here largely remained in family hands until the 1980s. The 1,826 acres eventually became a state park, which officially opened in 1991. The Penn family farm has been restored, and self-guided tours are available daily.

This trail is largely through open prairie, making it hot on a sunny day, so bring protection and plenty of water. The trail begins from the parking lot by a large sign. At about 0.15 mile veer right and continue through the tallgrass prairie. Cross a small bridge and bear left, going down a short hill. The trail winds down toward the lakeshore, eventually reaching a primitive camping area and chemical toilet.

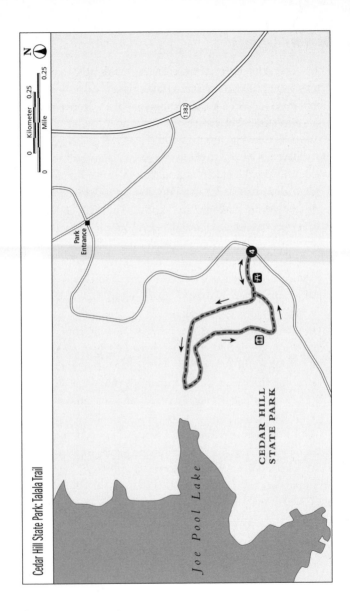

Cedar Hill State Park: Talala Trail

Miles and Directions

0.0 Start at the trailhead adjacent to the parking lot.

0.15 Veer right and continue through the tallgrass prairie.

0.2 Cross a creek on a wooden bridge and head downhill. (FYI: The creekbed may be dry.)

0.8 Skirt a treed area by the lakeshore and bear left toward a camping area.

1.0 Pass through a primitive campground.

1.3 Go left when the trail splits, heading uphill through the prairie toward the parking lot.

1.8 Arrive back at the trailhead.

5 Cedar Ridge Preserve: Cattail Pond Trail

This moderately challenging hike to one of the area's tallest peaks feels like it belongs in the Texas Hill Country. It can be surprisingly secluded given its central location in the Dallas–Fort Worth Metroplex. Unlike other area trails, which have little change in elevation, this one moves up and down like a roller coaster, offering thrilling views of Joe Pool Lake to the west and a calming moment or two by a cattail pond before winding back up to the trailhead.

Distance: 2.4 miles out and back

Approximate hiking time: 1 hour

Difficulty: More challenging

Trail surface: Packed dirt

Best season: Oct through Dec

Other trail users: Birders

Canine compatibility: Leashed dogs permitted

Fees and permits: Donations are appreciated, but there's no collection box. The Audubon Society accepts donations through its Web site.

Schedule: Preserve open 6:30 a.m. to 6:00 p.m. Nov 1 through Mar 31; 6:30 a.m. to 8:30 p.m. Apr 1 through Oct 31; closed Mon

Maps: TOPO! Texas CD; trail maps available from the Dallas Audubon Society on the Web site and at the visitors center

Trail contacts: Dallas Audubon Society; (972) 709-7784; www .audubondallas.org

Special considerations: The preserve has workdays on the third Saturday of every month. Volunteers, including many Boy Scout troops, perform trail maintenance and plant restoration.

No bicycles are permitted in the preserve.

Finding the trailhead: From I-20 take exit 458 to Mountain Creek Parkway and drive 2.8 miles. Cedar Ridge Preserve is on the right. The preserve's main drive leads to a gravel parking lot. A building with restrooms and posted trail signs are adjacent to the parking lot. Follow the main trail about 500 yards to the woods, where the Cattail Pond Trail begins. GPS: N32 38.276' / W96 57.531'

The Hike

Cedar Ridge Preserve is a not-for-profit natural habitat of 633 acres with 10 miles of hiking trails plus a butterfly garden and picnic area. Depending on the weekend, the preserve can feel crowded or blissfully remote.

The preserve's ten trails range in difficulty from the Little Bluestem Trail, a 0.25-mile wheelchair-accessible trail through a garden, to the Cedar Break Trail, a 1.7-mile up-and-down trek. You can vary the trails hiked on different visits, taking advantage of the time of year. The 1.0-mile Bluebonnet Trail is a perfect springtime pick, while the challenging Escarpment Trail is a great winter escape.

The Cattail Pond Trail is a great introduction to the preserve. The trail moves through scrubby woods with prickly pear cactus up to a prime peak, where hikers can pause to take in views to the west. The trail then travels down to the peaceful pond, where benches provide a midpoint picnic spot. It's also one of the best-marked trails in the preserve.

The trail begins next to the preserve's restrooms, by the butterfly garden. Veer right as the Possumhaw Trail splits off to the left near the trailhead. The trails rejoin just 0.3 mile farther, making for an interesting detour if time permits. Signs on the left warn of poisonous snakes, occasionally spotted on and along the trail, so keep an eye out.

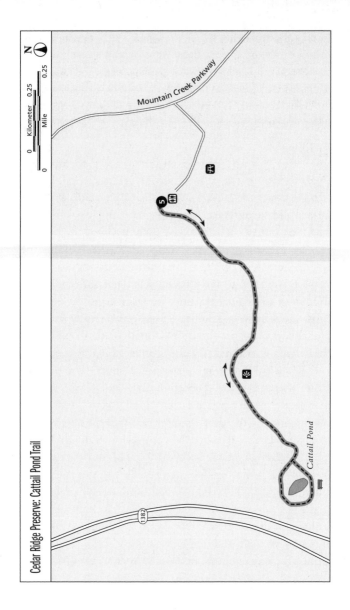

Cedar Ridge Preserve: Cattail Pond Trail

Mountain Creek Parkway

Cattail Pond

1382

N

Kilometer 0.25

Mile 0.25

At about 0.3 mile, the Cedar Break Trail branches to the left. Bear right to stay on the Cattail Pond Trail. The Cedar Break Trail also loops back to Cattail Pond, but it is more challenging and may be too difficult for families with young children. At about 1.0 mile there's a view of Joe Pool Lake before the trail goes down a steep ravine to the pond, the trail's turnaround spot.

Miles and Directions

0.0 Start on the trail next to butterfly garden, veering right at the intersection with Possumhaw Trail.

0.3 Possumhaw Trail rejoins on the left. Bear right to stay on the Cattail Pond Trail. Keep right when Cedar Break Trail splits off to left.

0.5 Stay right again when Cedar Break Trail rejoins the trail.

0.8 Veer right when Fossil Valley Trail splits off to the left.

1.0 Reach the overlook point before trail begins descent down to the pond.

1.2 Follow the trail around Cattail Pond and head back toward the trailhead.

2.4 Arrive back at the trailhead.

6 Breckenridge Park

This 417-acre park is a popular destination, particularly during soccer season, when the parking lots are jammed with local families toting tykes to weekend games. This hike makes the most of the park's 4.5 miles of trails, combining an out-and-back trail with a loop around the park's ten-acre lake.

Distance: 3.0-mile lollipop
Approximate hiking time: 1 to 1.5 hours
Difficulty: Easy
Trail surface: Paved
Best season: Mar through May, when the wildflowers are in bloom
Other trail users: Families use the park's wide trails to teach kids bike riding and to fish along the banks of the pond and adjacent Rowlett Creek.
Canine compatibility: Leashed dogs permitted
Fees and permits: No fees or permits required
Schedule: Park open daily sunrise to sunset

Maps: TOPO! Texas CD; trail maps available from Richardson Parks & Recreation. Pocket trail guides are available at Richardson City Hall, Heights Recreation Center, Huffhines Recreation Center, and the Senior Citizens Center.
Trail contacts: Richardson Parks & Recreation; (972) 744-4300; www.cor.net/parksandrecreation.aspx?id=3790/homepage.html
Special considerations: The city closes portions of the park after heavy rains.
In addition: Bring a camera for great shots of spring wildflowers and a pair of binoculars for bird watching.

Finding the trailhead: From Plano take President George Bush Turnpike east to the Renner Road exit. Turn left onto Renner. Travel north about 3 miles and turn right onto Brand Road. The park is located at 3300 Brand Rd. Turn right onto the entrance road, Park Vista Road, and follow it around to Parking Lot A. The trailhead is located directly across the road from the restrooms. GPS: N32 59.812' / W96 37.591'

The Hike

It's hard to believe this pastoral escape is partially built on an old city landfill. Luckily the land was reclaimed, and now Breckenridge Park serves as a much-needed respite from the daily grind and gridlock of the Telecom Corridor, a nickname derived from the high-tech firms that call Richardson and its neighboring cities home.

The park contains more than twenty-five acres of wildflowers and was the former home of the city's annual Wildflower! arts and music festival before the festival moved to the more urban Galatyn Park. Breckenridge Park is still the best viewing spot for the city's annual July 4 fireworks display.

On other days the loudest noises you'll hear are cheers from the dozen or so soccer fields, which draw area families for weekend games. To get to the trailhead, look for the primitive restroom facilities located by Parking Lot A. Cross the one-way street to the beginning of the paved trail. From here the trail heads down a gentle hill and away from the soccer fields.

When the trail splits, go right and cross a bridge over Rowlett Creek. The trail enters an open field and winds along the creek. Apart from soccer moms and dads, the park's noisiest residents will likely be found along this part of the trail—the ducks and swans that waddle along the creek's banks.

After passing under Renner Road, the trail dead-ends. Turn around here, making your way back by the creek and recrossing it.

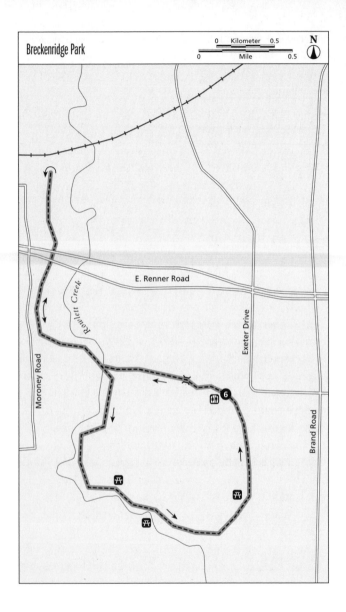

Breckenridge Park

E. Renner Road

Rowlett Creek

Moroney Road

Exeter Drive

Brand Road

Veer right at the trail split and then right again onto the trail that heads into the woods along the rushing waters of Rowlett Creek. Listen for woodpeckers, which frequent the cool, dense forest here.

The trail enters open space again, passing the park's ten-acre lake on the left. The lake is stocked with bass, catfish, perch, and crappie, but anglers have to adhere to the park's catch-and-release policy.

The trail winds around the lake, passing picnic pavilions and a playground before heading up a small hill back to the soccer fields and Parking Lot A.

Miles and Directions

0.0 Start at the trailhead and veer left downhill.

0.1 Go right at the trail junction. Cross a bridge and follow the trail into an open meadow along the creek.

0.5 The trail passes under East Renner Road.

0.7 The trail dead-ends. Turn around and circle back, retracing your route by the creek.

1.6 Go right at the trail junction and right again when the trail splits, heading into the woods surrounding Rowlett Creek.

1.9 Bear right at the trail juncture and pass a pond on the left.

2.5 Pass a picnic pavilion on the right and cross a bridge before looping back toward the parking lots.

3.0 Arrive back at the trailhead.

7 Spring Creek Preserve Trail

This trail winds through a dense forest that features some of the region's oldest trees, including some believed to be more than 300 years old. The preserve is the only spot in the world where eight different types of oaks grow together in one ecosystem, making it a favorite destination in late autumn. This level, paved trail leads to an overlook of a stream where turtles rest atop logs and woodpeckers hammer overhead.

Distance: 0.75 mile out and back

Approximate hiking time: 20 minutes

Difficulty: Easy

Trail surface: Paved

Best season: Oct through Dec

Other trail users: None

Canine compatibility: No dogs permitted

Fees and permits: No fees or permits required

Schedule: Preserve open daily 6:00 a.m. to 11:00 p.m.

Maps: TOPO! Texas CD

Trail contacts: Garland Parks and Recreation Department; (972) 205-3589

Society for the Preservation of Spring Creek; (972) 205-2750; www.springcreekforest.org

Special considerations: The trail is wheelchair accessible.

No bikes are allowed on the trail, making it one of the area's few paved yet bike-free trails.

Finding the trailhead: From Plano take the President George Bush Turnpike East to the Holford Road exit. Turn right (south) onto Holford Road and drive about 0.5 mile. The preserve entrance is on the left at 1770 Holford Rd. GPS: N32 57.864' / W96 39.183'

The Hike

This eighty-three-acre preserve just south of the President George Bush Turnpike in Garland gives a glimpse of what

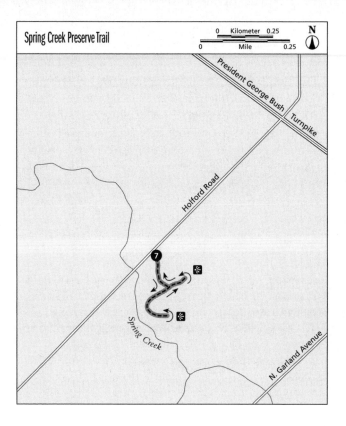

North Texas looked like before it was plowed and paved over. Located in the floodplain of Spring Creek, the preserve's towering overstory of trees includes eight species of oaks, most prominently chinquapin, Shumard, and bur. Wildlife commonly spotted along the trail include snails, lizards, and turtles parked atop partially submerged logs in the creek. This trail leads to a small viewing area of the creek, where you can relax under the dense canopy and take in the soothing sounds of the rushing water. Unfortunately litter also piles up in the stream, blemishing an otherwise idyllic experience with nature.

Well maintained by the Preservation Society for Spring Creek Forest, the trail is easily accessible for all ages and abilities. Those wanting more of a workout, and a bit more solitude, can head across Holford Road to the west side of the park, which features several longer and more primitive, unpaved trails and picnic tables for post-trek treats. This side of the park has younger trees, including short-lived cottonwoods and hackberry trees, and a less-dense canopy that allows for better wildflower blooms. Birders love the preserve, where commonly spotted species include Carolina wrens, tufted titmice, and various hawks.

Miles and Directions

0.0 Start at the parking lot. Look for a park sign listing rules and restrictions, and head to adjacent paved trail.

0.1 When the trail splits veer right. Follow the trail farther into woods, where it winds along a stream.

0.3 The trail dead-ends at a stream. Turn around and follow the path back to the split.

0.5 The trail divides. Continue straight to reach a lookout point offering a view of the stream. Turn back and veer right to return to the parking lot.

0.75 Arrive back at the parking lot.

8 Arbor Hills Loop

Popular with families, scout troops, hikers, and geocachers, this trail winds uphill through woods and blackland prairie culminating in a hilltop view of Plano and its surroundings before looping back to the trailhead.

Distance: 2.3-mile loop
Approximate hiking time: 1 hour
Difficulty: Easy
Trail surface: Paved path
Best season: Apr through May
Other users: Some cyclists and in-line skaters; mountain bikers typically head for dirt trails that sprout off the side of the main trail.
Canine compatibility: Leashed dogs permitted
Schedule: Park open daily 5:00 a.m. to 11:00 p.m.

Maps: TOPO! Texas CD; map available online at http://pdf .plano.gov/parks/ArborHills.pdf
Trail contacts: Plano Parks and Recreation; (972) 941-7788 (recorded information); www .plano.gov/Departments/parksand recreation/Pages/default.aspx
Special considerations: The 1.0-mile loop from the park entrance to the observation tower typically takes 15 to 20 minutes if you want to time it to take in the view at sunrise or sunset.

Finding the trailhead: From Dallas take the Dallas North Tollway to the Parker Road exit. Turn left onto Parker Road and travel 1 mile. The preserve is on the right, just past Midway Road at 6701 West Parker Rd. GPS: N33 02.800' / W96 50.907'

The Hike

Just a few miles from the corporate headquarters of JCPenney and Frito-Lay, this 200-acre park offers more than 2.2 miles of paved trails; plenty of unpaved alternative routes to

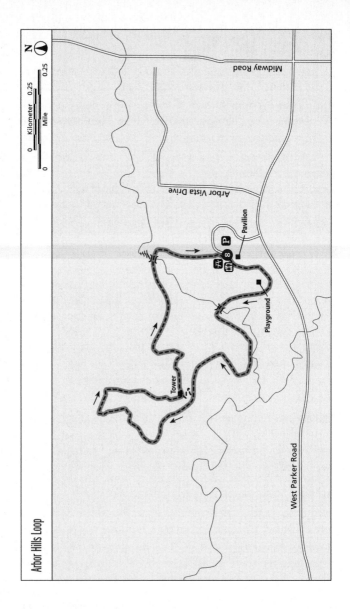

Arbor Hills Loop

escape urban living; and, of all things, a hill amidst the city's famously flat terrain.

From the parking lot, head to the large stone pavilion at the entrance, where picnic tables and restrooms are available. There's a large map of all the park's trails, both paved and unpaved, on the right wall of the pavilion across from the restrooms and more information about the diverse ecosystems in the park, including riparian wetlands, blackland prairie, and upland forest.

On most weekends the park is jammed with families taking to the paved trails with strollers, scooters, bikes, and in-line skates. Mountain bikers also flock to the park and its network of unpaved trails. While hikers are welcomed to use the unpaved trails, they are typically closed for several days after rains.

From the entrance pavilion the trail heads down a slight incline, passing a playground on the right. The trail then moves into a forest and crosses over a small stream before heading through blackland prairie, so named for the gumbo-like soil. This thick and dense medium provides the perfect home to an abundant variety of wildflowers, including the yellow-and-red Mexican hatband and bluebonnets, the official state flower of Texas. Both typically bloom late March through April.

From the main trail you'll take a left and hit the Tower Trail. Head up the hill toward the large stone observation tower. A shortcut to the tower is available on the right, but stay straight and enter the forest. Slowly wind up the hill behind the tower; veer left at the fork near the top of the hill and continue toward the tower. Consider timing your hike to hit the tower at sunrise or sunset for a memorable view of the park and its surrounding subdivisions and office high-rises.

From the tower head back downhill. Bear right to get back on the trail and then reenter the prairie, where you'll see the main trail. Go left and head into the forest. Cross a bridge over India Creek; if you look to the right, you'll see a small waterfall.

At the 2.0-mile mark the trail splits. Veer right and head back up to the parking lot and trailhead.

Miles and Directions

0.0 Start at the large stone pavilion and picnic area adjacent to the parking lot and turn left onto the trail.

0.2 Pass a playground on the right.

0.3 Head straight into the forest and cross a bridge.

0.6 Bear left and head uphill toward the tower.

0.8 Go left at the trail junction, heading into the forest.

1.3 Veer left when the trail splits and head to the tower.

1.5 Take in the view from the tower before retracing your steps and turning left onto the main trail.

1.6 Veer left when the trail intersects another paved path, and head into the forest.

1.7 Cross a bridge, looking to the right to take in a waterfall.

2.0 Veer right when the trail splits, heading into an opening by the parking lot.

2.3 Arrive back at the trailhead.

9 Heard Wildlife Sanctuary: Wood Duck Trail

This comprehensive nature preserve is well worth the drive. The sanctuary offers a museum and a small zoo along with a wide variety of trails through wetlands, prairies, and forests. Educational markers identify plants and encourage conservation.

Distance: 3.5-mile lollipop
Approximate hiking time: 1.5 hours
Difficulty: Moderate; can be more challenging after rain, when trails are slippery
Trail surface: Packed gravel; some portions on a wooden boardwalk with rails
Best season: Mar through May
Other trail users: The sanctuary operates nature education classes for children and is a popular field trip destination.
Canine compatibility: Dogs not permitted

Fees and permits: Entrance fee; no charge for children under 3
Schedule: Sanctuary open Mon through Sat 9:00 a.m. to 5:00 p.m.; Sun 1:00 to 5:00 p.m.
Maps: TOPO! Texas CD; printed maps available at the education center
Trail contacts: The Heard Natural Science Museum & Wildlife Sanctuary; (972) 562-5566; www.heardmuseum.org
Special considerations: Trails are open only during museum hours, but guided night hikes are available for $12 per person. Call for more information.

Finding the trailhead: Take US 75 north from Dallas to McKinney and travel to exit 38A. Proceed east on TX 5 for 0.75 mile. Turn left onto FM 1378 and drive approximately 1 mile to the museum entrance on left. GPS: N33 09.554' / W96 36.913'

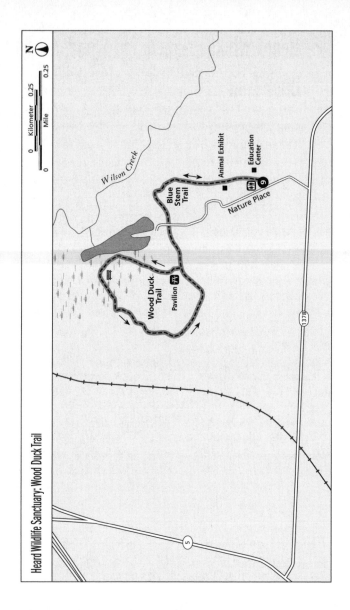

Heard Wildlife Sanctuary: Wood Duck Trail

The Hike

Bessie Heard was born in 1886, the eldest of five daughters of one of Collin County's founding families. She never married but instead poured her energy into civic pursuits, including establishing this museum and sanctuary in 1964. She died in 1988 at the age of 101. Miss Bess, as she was affectionately known, was passionate about encouraging children's love of nature, and her legacy continues to grow with the facility's ever-expanding array of exhibits and events.

Kids will love the 25,000-square-foot education center with its exhibits on dinosaurs, snakes, and geodes. The 289-acre center offers more than 6.5 miles of trails and is home to more than 240 species of animals. You might catch a glimpse of flying squirrels, alligator snapping turtles, and the occasional bobcat.

A sign as you enter the trail warns about the dangers of copperhead snakes, whose reddish brown color can blend in with the sandy dirt trail. Keep an eye out as you walk for snakes that may be sunning themselves on the trail.

To sample a variety of ecosystems, this hike combines the 1.0-mile Bluestem Trail, named for a grass that grows to 4 feet tall, and the 1.0-mile Wood Duck Trail.

From the education center, exit to the back patio and look for the trail marker. Veer left and head toward the center's outdoor animal exhibits. True to its sanctuary designation, Heard provides a home for wayward and injured animals, including several exotic species as well as Texas natives. There's also a new butterfly garden.

Detour through the exhibits and pick up the trail again, veering right into the blackland prairie. Here an educational marker explains that Texas has retained only a tiny fraction—less than 0.04 percent—of the twelve million acres of blackland prairie that once covered the state. The trail winds through a forested wetland and becomes a boardwalk over the mud. The Bluestem Trail ends near a large picnic pavilion. Go right and pick up the Wood Duck Trail, a boardwalk over a pond where several benches provide ideal spots for wildlife watching. The trail curves back around to rejoin the Bluestem Trail. Turn around and retrace your steps back to the education center.

Miles and Directions

0.0 Start at the education center. Walk through to the back and exit onto the terrace. Look for signs labeling the Bluestem Trail to the left and walk into woods.

0.1 Come to a small zoo area on the left. Detour through the exhibits or continue along the main trail.

0.5 Cross a gravel service road and continue straight into the woods.

0.7 Bear right onto the Wood Duck Trail and head toward a pond.

1.0 Cross another service road and continue on a boardwalk over the pond.

1.4 Cross a road and follow the trail back into forest.

1.6 Cross a service road and head into open prairie area.

1.7 Turn right to pick up the Bluestem Trail and head back to the education center.

3.5 Arrive back at the trailhead.

10 L. B. Houston Nature Trail

This trail is largely for off-road cycling, but hikers are welcome as long as they give cyclists right-of-way. Located just off TX 114 in Irving, the trail winds through a leafy glade and then offers a prime picnic spot by the Elm Fork of the Trinity River.

Distance: 1.6-mile loop

Approximate hiking time: 1 hour

Difficulty: Easy, if you don't mind making way for mountain bikers

Trail surface: Dirt

Best season: May through July

Other users: Trail maintained by and for off-road cyclists

Canine compatibility: Not recommended for dogs; hikers frequently have to move aside for cyclists and the trail is narrow in many areas.

Fees and permits: No fees or permits required

Schedule: Sunrise to sunset

Maps: TOPO! Texas CD

Trail contacts: Trail maintained by the Dallas Off Road Bicycling Association (DORBA); www .dorba.org

Special considerations: The trail is closed for several days after a heavy rain. Check the DORBA Web site for the latest conditions before heading out.

There are special workdays for trail maintenance, usually the last Sunday of the month during which time portions of the trail might be closed.

There is no water available on the trail, so be sure to bring what you need.

Finding the trailhead: The park is located on California Crossing off TX 114 in Irving. From Dallas, take TX 114 west toward Dallas/ Fort Worth International Airport. Exit at O'Connor Boulevard. Head right, then turn right on Riverside Drive. Turn left onto California Crossing and look for a gravel parking lot on the right. GPS: N32 51.999' / W96 55.433'

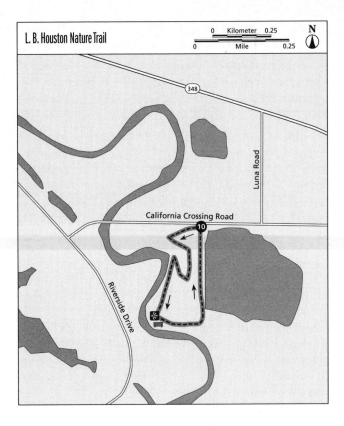

L. B. Houston Nature Trail

0 Kilometer 0.25
0 Mile 0.25

N

348

Luna Road

California Crossing Road

10

Riverside Drive

The Hike

The trail takes you on a winding path through a dense forest by the Trinity River, including a great riverside resting spot to check out turtles, snakes, and herons. Maintained by the Dallas Off Road Bicycle Association (DORBA), the park is overcoming its shady reputation as a drinking spot. (It is located not far from liquor stores at the Dallas city limits on Northwest Highway.)

With more than 7.0 miles of singletrack trails, the park is a major draw for cyclists testing their skill and nerves on the winding paths. There's a pond by the parking lot, where local anglers like to try their luck. Look for the park regulations posted on a small billboard; the trailhead is to the right. The loop is designed to be done counterclockwise, so start the trail by turning right and moving into the forest. Here the very dense growth of privet feels almost junglelike, which no doubt adds to the challenge of biking it. But for hikers it's just a matter of watching for low-lying branches and listening for cyclists coming up from behind—they get the right of way here.

The narrow trail often has room for only single-file hiking as it meanders toward the river. At the 1.0-mile mark there's a small bench for taking in the view, but unfortunately there's not a lot of other room along the trail here.

Despite being surrounded by major freeways and bustling high-rises of Las Colinas, the park has abundant wildlife, with butterflies and birds flitting in and out of the tree canopy down to the river. The trail crosses a small bridge and enters an open meadow at about 1.4 miles. From here you can see the trailhead; turn left and follow the dirt road back to the parking lot.

Miles and Directions

0.0 Start at the trailhead to the right of the billboard and turn right onto the trail.

0.1 The trail heads into woods, tightly winding in hairpin curves.

1.0 Come to the Trinity River Overlook.

1.4 Veer left, heading toward an open meadow. Picking up a two-lane dirt road, turn left to return to the trailhead.

1.6 Arrive back at the trailhead.

11 Little Bear Creek Trail

A popular dog park adjacent to this trail makes it ideal for canines. Educational markers identifying various tree species, a scenic dock overlooking a large pond, and well-maintained fields and a playground make for an enjoyable outing for kids and adults alike.

Distance: 2.0 miles out and back

Approximate hiking time: 1 hour

Difficulty: Easy

Trail surface: Mostly paved path; some gravel and dirt path sections

Best season: Feb through May

Other users: Cyclists, runners, and dog walkers

Canine compatibility: Leashed dogs permitted

Schedule: Park open daily 7:00 a.m. to 11:00 p.m.

Maps: TOPO! Texas CD; map available online at www.euless .org/pacs/trails.htm

Trail contacts: City of Euless Parks and Recreation Department; (817) 685-1429

Special considerations: The park's fields are very popular on weekends for soccer and flag football games. The dog park also draws crowds, so parking can be a pain.

Finding the trailhead: From Dallas, take Airport Freeway (also called Texas Highway 183) then take Texas Highway 360 north and exit at Mid-Cities Boulevard. Turn left heading west onto Mid-Cities Boulevard and go about a half mile. Turn left at Bear Creek Parkway. The park is about 0.25 mile on the right. The trailhead is by the parking lot, next to the dog park. GPS: N32 51.901' / W97 04.156'

The Hike

Just a couple of miles west of Dallas/Fort Worth International Airport, this trail follows Little Bear Creek just before

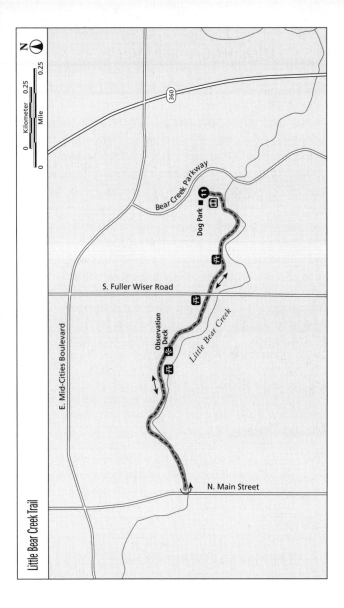

Little Bear Creek Trail

N

0 Kilometer 0.25

0 Mile 0.25

360

Bear Creek Parkway

Dog Park

S. Fuller Wiser Road

E. Mid-Cities Boulevard

Observation Deck

Little Bear Creek

N. Main Street

it meets up with Big Bear Creek and meanders along a tree-lined greenbelt through two city parks. The four-acre dog park means lots of canines are typically walking along the paths, and waste bags and periodic dumping stations are provided along the trail.

Start the trail by the main parking lot next to the dog park and head toward the tree-lined creek area. Veer left off the paved path onto the gravel trail for a walk along the creekbanks on the Texas Outdoor Education Trail, with its detailed descriptions of the various tree species seen along the trail. Signs that read BEAR CROSSING don't refer to actual bears but are spots where paths cross over Little Bear Creek. Several dirt trails spring off the main trail and lead down to the creek for a closer look. At about 0.25 mile the trail enters a more open area alongside playing fields. At about 0.5 mile veer left toward a pond with an observation deck— a nice birding spot—and then rejoin the main trail.

Follow the wide paved path along the creek until you reach the spot where Main Street crosses over the trail. This is the turnaround. If you want to hike a bit farther, the trail continues through Bob Eden Park. You can add another 1.0 mile to the hike, turning around at the playground there.

Miles and Directions

0.0   Start from the parking lot by the dog park. The trailhead is located where the paved path heads toward a tree-lined creek.

0.25 Bear right as the trail enters an open area by playing fields.

0.5   Veer left, walking down to an observation deck over pond.

1.0   The trail passes under Main Street, your turnaround point. Retrace your steps back to the trailhead.

2.0   Arrive back at the trailhead.

12 Lake Grapevine Horseshoe Trail

This hike takes advantage of streets closed to traffic to enjoy a wide pathway through a post oak forest and to great views of Lake Grapevine. The trail goes past soccer fields, baseball diamonds, and a picnic pavilion, ending at a lakeside playground, making it a great outing for children.

Distance: 4.5 miles out and back

Approximate hiking time: 2 hours

Difficulty: Easy

Trail surface: Paved

Best season: Year-round

Other trail users: Cyclists, in-line skaters

Canine compatibility: Leashed dogs permitted

Fees and permits: No fees or permits required

Schedule: Park open daily 6:00 a.m. to 9:00 p.m.

Maps: TOPO! Texas CD; maps available online at www.grape vinetexas.gov

Trail contacts: City of Grapevine Parks and Recreation Department; (817) 410-3450; www .grapevinetexas.gov

Special considerations: This hike is gorgeous around sunset. Cabins and campsites are available at the Vineyards campground, which also offers kayak rentals and a geocaching program. For more information call (817) 329-8993 or visit www .vineyardscampground.com.

Finding the trailhead: Take TX 114 west from Dallas to Grapevine and exit at Park Boulevard, bearing right at the fork to stay on Park. Drive about 1 mile to intersection with Dove Road and turn left onto Dove. The parking lot for the trail is about 0.25 mile on the right. GPS: N32 57.345' / W97 06.308'

Lake Grapevine Horseshoe Trail

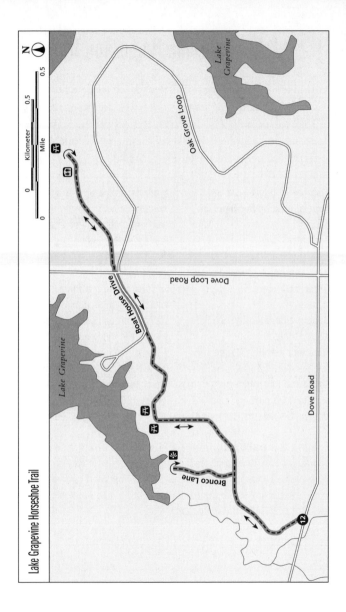

The Hike

Located on the south side of Lake Grapevine, which supplies water for Highland and University Park as well as portions of the city of Grapevine, this trail is only a few miles from bustling Grapevine Mills, Dallas/Fort Worth International Airport, and the massive Gaylord Texan resort. Thanks to those developments and others, the city enjoys a healthy tax base and offers first-rate parks, including this well-tended trail.

The first part of the hike, about 1.5 miles, is on an old paved park road that's now open only to foot and bike traffic. Off-road cyclists take to side dirt trails that branch off the main trail.

The trail starts from the parking lot off Dove Road and then heads through a grassy opening, passing houses on the right and Little Bear Creek down the hill on the left. The trail then curves right.

At the junction with Bronco Lane, the trail follows the cul-de-sac down to the water's edge for a good view of the lake. The trail then heads back up the street to pick up the main road, bearing left and heading downhill for another view of the lake on the left. The trail surface becomes concrete and heads up a hill, crossing over Dove Loop Road and into a post oak forest where squirrels scamper.

The trail enters Oak Grove Park, a hub of baseball and soccer fields and plenty of picnic tables filled with families on sunny weekends. A lakeside playground and nearby water fountains and restrooms make a nice resting spot before turning around and heading back to the trailhead.

Miles and Directions

0.0 Start at the trail sign at the back of the parking lot. Stay on the wide paved street when you come to junctions with concrete-paved and dirt paths.

0.5 Take Bronco Lane left to the end of the cul-de-sac. Retrace your steps after viewing the lake.

0.8 Rejoin the main trail. Turn left and follow the road as it winds downhill with the lake on the left.

1.2 Cross Dove Loop Road, and follow the path as it leads into the woods.

1.8 Stay on the trail as it emerges from woods to an open area with soccer fields overlooking Lake Grapevine.

2.25 The trail reaches a playground, your turnaround point. Retrace your steps back to trailhead.

4.5 Arrive back at the trailhead.

13 Walnut Grove Trail

This 3-mile trail hugs the south shore of Lake Grapevine, offering stunning views and surprising solitude. The first part of the trail is through woods; the second part is along the shoreline. The trail is open to horses and restricted to mountain bikers, but they sometimes can't resist. Be prepared to see a few fat tire marks along with tracks of armadillos, opossums, and the occasional coyote.

Distance: 3.0 miles out and back
Approximate hiking time: 2 hours
Difficulty: Moderate to more challenging
Trail surface: Packed dirt and sand
Best season: Mar through May; Nov through Dec
Other users: Equestrians
Canine compatibility: Leashed dogs permitted
Fees and permits: No fees or permits required
Schedule: Park open sunrise to sunset
Maps: TOPO! Texas CD; maps available from Southlake Parks and Recreation online at www.southlakeparks.com or at the city's parks office
Trail contacts: U.S. Army Corps of Engineers; (817) 865-2600; http://www.swf-wc.usace.army.mil/grapevine/index.asp
City of Southlake; www.southlakeparks.com
Special considerations: Since this is an equestrian trail, look out for horse droppings and be sure to give equestrians the right-of-way. Since shoes can sink in the sand along the beach, wear older boots.
There is no water available on the trail, so bring what you need.

Finding the trailhead: From Dallas take TX 114 west to the White Chapel Boulevard exit. Drive north 3 miles to where the road ends at a parking lot. The trailhead is adjacent to the parking lot's east side. GPS: N33 00.278' / W97 09.433'

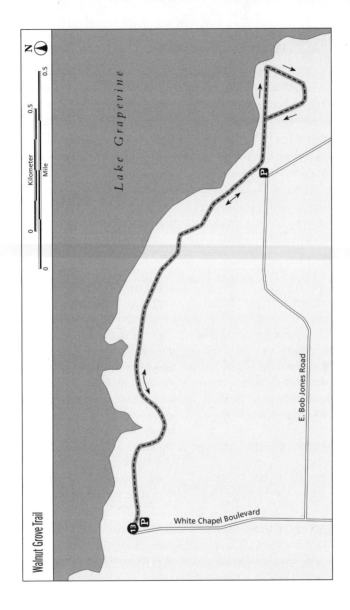

Walnut Grove Trail

Lake Grapevine

N

Kilometer
0   0.5
Mile
0   0.5

E. Bob Jones Road

White Chapel Boulevard

13

The Hike

A series of interconnecting loops make it easy to shorten or lengthen this hike along the shore of Lake Grapevine. Despite being a few miles west of Dallas/Fort Worth International Airport, the park feels very remote. For simplicity, this trail hugs the shoreline of Lake Grapevine and the lake's sandy beach can provide a good workout and somewhat muddy shoes, depending on recent rainfall.

Because several trails spring off the main trail, it can be challenging to follow the main trail, but simply simply keep your eye to the shoreline to avoid getting too far offtrack.

The trailhead is the low gate entrance to the right side of the parking lot. Here the dirt trail winds through a tallgrass meadow. At about 0.5 mile the trail comes to another parking lot on the right.

The trail splits, passing several tall bird boxes on its way toward the beach. Simply follow the shoreline, watching the occasional fisherman trolling in the more remote part of the lake in search of bass, catfish, and crappies. On the lakeshore you'll see freshwater oyster shells and driftwood and may spot tracks from opossums, raccoons, and the pack of coyotes known to roam here.

Equestrians are another common sight, as this is a popular trail ride for nearby Marshall Creek Ranch. Follow the shoreline to the point that juts out to reveal the next cove, about 2.5 miles from where you started. Turn around here and retrace the shoreline back to the trailhead.

Miles and Directions

0.0 Start at the trailhead on the east side of the parking lot.
0.5 Head right when the trail splits.

0.7 As the side trail springs off, stay straight, heading along the shoreline.

1.2 Pass another parking lot on the right. Bear left at the fork and follow the trail to the lakeshore.

1.5 Reach a peninsula jutting out in the lake. Turn around and retrace your path.

3.0 Arrive back at the trailhead.

14 Bob Jones Nature Center Trail

This short loop through woods, fields, and wetlands is ideal for families with small children. The adjacent nature center features hands-on exhibits, educational programs, and a gift shop.

Distance: 0.75-mile loop
Approximate hiking time: 30 minutes
Difficulty: Easy
Trail surface: Packed dirt
Best season: Mar through June; Oct through Dec
Other trail users: None
Canine compatibility: No dogs permitted
Fees and permits: No fees or permits required
Schedule: Park open daily from dawn to dusk; nature center open Tues through Sat 9:00 a.m. to 5:00 p.m.
Maps: TOPO! Texas CD
Trail contacts: Bob Jones Nature Center; (817) 491-6333; www.bjnc.org
Special considerations: There are several great picnic spots along the trail, and be sure to stop by the nature center to view the wildlife exhibits. Early morning is the best time to see wildlife, including deer and wild turkeys.

Finding the trailhead: From Dallas take TX 114 west to the White Chapel Boulevard exit. Drive north for 2.5 miles to the intersection with Bob Jones Road. Turn right onto Bob Jones Road; the nature center is on left. The trailhead is just to the left of the nature center building. GPS: N32 59.825' / W97 09.168'

The Hike

The Bob Jones Nature Center opened in 2008 on land owned by Jones—who was born a slave and lived in the area, eventually owning more than 2,000 acres. Now part

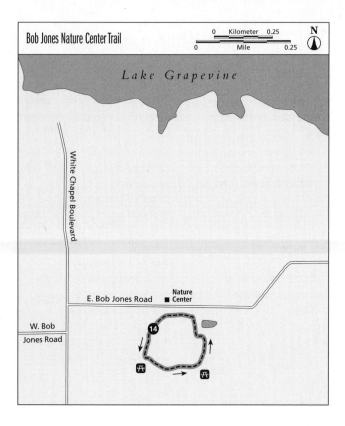

0   Kilometer   0.25

0   Mile   0.25

N

Lake Grapevine

White Chapel Boulevard

E. Bob Jones Road

Nature Center

W. Bob Jones Road

14

of the City of Southlake's parks system, the grounds cover nearly 500 acres of wildlife habitat along the shores of Lake Grapevine. To encourage wildlife, dogs and horses are prohibited on this trail.

Still largely undiscovered, the center and this hike make for a great afternoon family outing. The nature center building includes a small gift shop, where you can buy butterfly nets, birdcalls, and other kid-friendly gear. There's also a small animal display that includes several snakes and lizards, plus a water fountain and restrooms. On weekends and during summer, the center offers hands-on nature programs for kids.

This short loop showcases the diverse ecosystem of the Eastern Cross Timbers, a slim strip of oak and elm woodlands stretching from the Red River south to Waco.

The trail begins by a picnic shelter south of the Bob Jones Nature Center and circles through woods, open fields, and a small pond. There are three picnic tables located along the trail. About 0.6 mile into the trail, there's a small pond and viewing area where you can occasionally spot ducks. While this trail offers a short, easy hike, it can be combined with the nearby Walnut Grove Trail to offer a full day of more intense hiking.

Miles and Directions

0.0 Start from the nature center parking lot and head toward the picnic pavilion.

0.3 Follow the trail as it circles past a picnic table.

0.6 Pass the pond and wildlife observation area.

0.75 Wind your way back, moving slightly uphill to arrive back at the nature center.

15 Colleyville Nature Center Trail

This flat, wooded trail begins by a small playground and picnic pavilion and winds along a bubbling creek through a riparian forest and wetlands and past ponds. The ponds are home to an impressive variety of birds, including the great blue heron and its smaller relative, the green heron, plus flocks of mallards and the forty-six-acre park's resident gaggle of geese.

Distance: 1.25-mile loop

Approximate hiking time: 30 minutes

Difficulty: Easy

Trail surface: Begins with paved path and then becomes dirt path for majority of trail

Best season: Winter for fewer crowds; spring for best birding and wildlife viewing

Other trail users: Mountain bikers, neighborhood families, and dog walkers

Canine compatibility: Leashed dogs permitted

Fees and permits: No fees or permits required

Schedule: Park open daily from 30 minutes before sunrise to 30 minutes after sunset

Maps: TOPO! Texas CD; detailed trail map available through the city of Colleyville Parks and Recreation Department by calling (817) 656-7275

Trail contacts: Colleyville Parks and Recreation Department; (817) 656-7275; www .colleyville.com/content/ view/38/422/

Special considerations: Parts of the trail wind close to neighborhood homes. After a very heavy rain, the creek can turn into a raging river.

Bring binoculars for bird watching, or enjoy catch-and-release fishing from the park's fishing pier.

Finding the trailhead: From Northeast Loop I-820 in North Richland Hills, take the TX 26/Grapevine Highway exit. Follow TX 26 northeast for 4.8 miles. Turn left onto Glade Road and proceed 0.6 mile to Mill Creek Drive. Turn left and follow Mill Creek Drive through a subdivision for 0.3 mile. The park's playground and picnic pavilion are located by the intersection of Mill Creek and Mill Wood Drives. Turn left into the parking area and look for large sign reading COL-LEYVILLE NATURE CENTER. GPS: N32 52.459' / W97 10.100'

The Hike

The Colleyville Nature Center and its system of more than 3.0 miles of trails is a relaxing retreat for Mid-Cities residents and bird watchers. More than twenty varieties of warblers have been recorded here, including golden-winged and hooded warblers. The trail has several shaded picnic tables and an adjacent playground, making it a great hike for parents with young children or anyone looking to walk off a meal.

The Nature Trail is the main trail in the park, but other short trails join and connect it in various spots, making it easy to shorten or lengthen your hike as desired. Much of the trail winds along Little Bear Creek, which joins Big Bear Creek near the Dallas/Fort Worth International Airport before flowing into the West Fork of the Trinity River. Several years ago, some residents reported seeing a panther along the creek's banks, but officials never confirmed the sightings. Still, local lore did prompt the high school to name its sports teams the Colleyville Panthers.

You'll begin the hike on a paved trail by the parking lot and then head into a dense forest of post oak, cotton-wood, American elm, pecan, and sugar hackberry trees. The trail crosses a bridge over Little Bear Creek by an outdoor

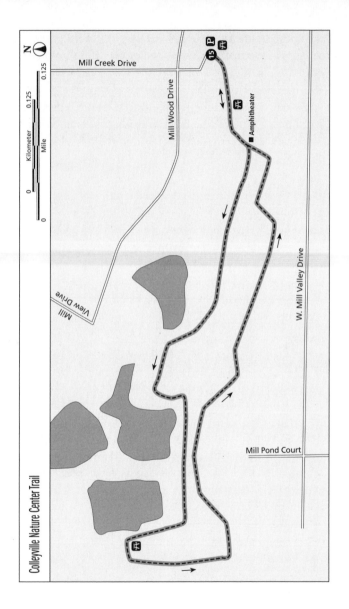

Colleyville Nature Center Trail

Mill Creek Drive

Mill Wood Drive

Mill View Drive

W. Mill Valley Drive

Mill Pond Court

Amphitheater

15

P

N

Kilometer
0   0.125

Mile
0   0.125

amphitheater and winds along the creek for 0.25 mile before reaching an open grassy area by the ponds. Here you may spot herons, kingfishers, and flycatchers, as well as flocks of ducks and the park's resident gaggle of noisy geese.

The trail circles around the ponds and then reenters the forest. Cross back over the creek and meet the trail back at the amphitheater. From here you can spot the parking lot and return to the trailhead.

Miles and Directions

0.0 Start at the COLLEYVILLE NATURE CENTER marker and take paved path into the woods.

0.22 Look for a marker with map of park trails. Follow the paved path toward the woods as it becomes a dirt trail.

0.3 Cross over Little Bear Creek on a bridge and go by an outdoor amphitheater.

0.5 The trail enters a grassy meadow by ponds.

0.8 The trail loops back toward a wooded area.

1.0 Cross the bridge and pass back by the amphitheater. Follow the trail back to the parking lot.

1.25 Arrive back at the parking lot.

16 River Legacy Park Trail

This flat, paved trail is popular with runners, cyclists, and hikers alike. The 1,300-acre park includes 8.0 miles of trails along the West Fork of the Trinity River, where the river's steep banks are lined with mature bottomland hardwoods that draw abundant wildlife. This hike covers the west side of the park, where the trail is shaded by massive gnarled oaks and is a bit less traveled, perhaps due to the adjacent sewage treatment facility. A bench perched by the riverbank provides a nice midhike picnic spot.

Distance: 3.2 miles out and back
Approximate hiking time: 1.5 hours
Difficulty: Easy
Trail surface: Concrete pavement
Best season: Feb through May; Oct through Dec
Other trail users: Cyclists, in-line skaters, and runners
Canine compatibility: Leashed dogs permitted
Fees and permits: No fees or permits required
Schedule: Park open daily 5:00 a.m. to 10:00 p.m.; science center open Tues through Sat 9:00 a.m. to 5:00 p.m.
Maps: TOPO! Texas CD; sign with trail maps at park entrance; map available online at www.river legacy.org
Trail contacts: Arlington Parks and Recreation; (817) 459-5473
Special considerations: The park's Living Science Center is a great stop before hitting the trail. Pick up brochures identifying the different plants and animals in the park, including a handy handout on animal tracks.
Water fountains and restrooms are available at the trailhead.

Finding the trailhead: From Dallas, take Interstate 30 west to Cooper Street exit. Head north to Northwest Green Oaks Boulevard. Turn left onto Green Oaks and go 0.25 mile to the entrance of

River Legacy Park. Follow the park drive to the end. The trailhead is located by the parking lot. GPS: N32 47.508' / W97 06.764'

The Hike

River Legacy Park is a major destination for Arlington-area residents year-round, including special events such as spring's Cardboard Boat Regatta. Its Living Science Center contains informative exhibits on natural history and native plants and animals, as well as tips on living green. In fact, much of the center itself was constructed using sustainable design and largely built from recycled materials.

The trailhead is located at the end of the park's drive west of the Living Science Center, making a visit to the center an easy addition to the hike. Several small trails branch off from the park's main trail along the Trinity River here. From the parking lot, take the concrete path at the back of the lot and head into the woods. The path connects with the main park trail in about 100 yards by a large wooden bridge.

If time permits, take a brief detour. Bear to the right where the trail from the parking lot meets the larger main trail and cross a bridge over Snider Legacy Creek to quickly check out a dense thicket of trees that's home to a colony of spiders. After viewing the arachnids, turn around and head west on the main trail.

The wide trail winds along the river, on the right. The park's picnic tables and fields are on the left. Veer right at a fork, staying on the main trail as it continues along the river. The city's sewage treatment center is located just on the other side of the river here, so smells related to processing the residue of more than 300,000 people waft over the trail. The churning sounds of a natural gas well may also be heard. The trail passes over deposits of Barnett shale, a rich

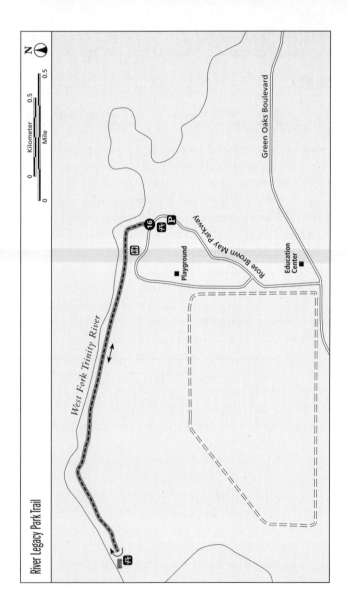

River Legacy Park Trail

underground reservoir of natural gas and some oil that lies under much of the region. The paved trail ends at 1.6 miles, where a picnic spot by the river provides a place to relax and take in the wildlife before heading back to the trailhead.

Miles and Directions

0.0   Start at the science center parking lot. After 30 yards veer right, heading through the woods. Look for the wide, well-marked main trail.

0.1   Go left when you meet up with the main trail.

0.5   Bear right at the fork to stay on the main trail, following the river

1.6   The trail ends; retrace your steps back to the parking lot.

3.2   Arrive back at the parking lot.

17 North Shore Trail

This trail gets its name from its location—the north shore of Lake Grapevine—and is a favorite among Dallas/Fort Worth hikers, runners, and cyclists. The trail has lots of rocks and roots and lots of ups and downs, but nothing too steep. Sunny weekends can bring crowded trails as nature lovers come to take in the lake views from the trail's cliffs.

Distance: 6.1 miles out and back

Approximate hiking time: 2.5 hours

Difficulty: Moderate

Trail surface: Dirt, some paved concrete

Best season: Mar through Sep

Other trail users: Mountain bikers and runners

Canine compatibility: Leashed dogs permitted

Fees and permits: No fees or permits required

Schedule: Park open daily sunrise to sunset

Maps: TOPO! Texas CD

Trail contacts: U.S. Army Corps of Engineers; (817) 865-2600; http://www.swf-wc.usace.army .mil/grapevine/index.asp

Special considerations: Some portions of the trail may be underwater if lake levels are above normal. Water is turned off in winter to prevent freezing.

Finding the trailhead: From TX 121 north, take the Bass Pro Drive exit and turn left. Head west to a stoplight. Drive ahead to the Northwest Highway (after two lights) and turn left again, heading south. Drive for approximately 0.5 mile and turn right (west) onto Fairway Drive. Drive across the Lake Grapevine dam and then over the spillway. After 0.25 mile you will see the Concourse Golf Course on the right and the entrance to Rockledge Park on the left. Turn left into Rockledge Park and then right at the first fork in the road. Drive all the way past the restroom facilities (which are on your right) to the edge of the lake directly in front of the trailhead. GPS: N32 58.975' / W97 04.058'

The Hike

One of the most popular—if not the most popular—hikes in the region, this trail can sometimes feel loved to death. Conditions are crowded on many weekends. Mountain bikers flock here. You'll have to share the trail with them for most of the stretches, so be listening for wheels crunching behind you.

The hike starts off at Rockledge Park and winds over cliffside trails overlooking Lake Grapevine. Avoid this trail after a heavy rain, when it's muddy and sometimes impassable as the lake overtakes its banks. You're just a few miles north of Dallas/Fort Worth International Airport, so be ready for the shadows of largebody planes to hover overhead through portions of this hike.

The area is also home to fossils, and some were found a few years ago when lake levels were very low. Due to damage by vandals, the fossils were covered up by the U.S. Army Corps of Engineers, which oversees this lake and its watershed, and their location is kept secret.

The trailhead is located by the parking lot. Enter the trail and head up a small hill to reach the lakeshore. Follow the shoreline to reach a series of cliffs. The path then meanders away from the lake slightly, still providing an occasional glimpse of water as it enters the forest. Bear right at the first two forks you encounter. At the 1.0-mile mark, cross a small bridge and go right when the trail widens out a bit. At 1.2 miles there's a scenic overlook before the trail heads into a grassy meadow. This is a good place to turn back if you want to shorten your hike.

At 1.6 miles you will cross over a road and head into a picnic area. Pick up the trail as it heads back into the woods.

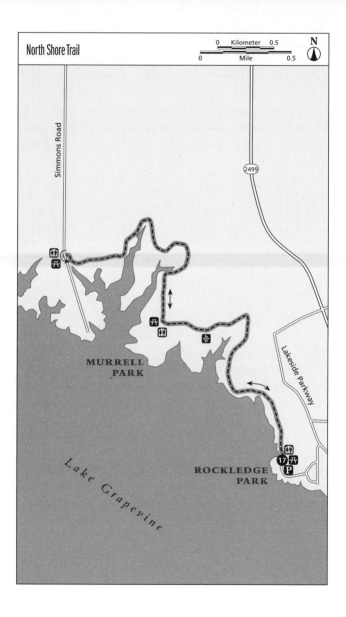

North Shore Trail

Simmons Road

2499

MURRELL PARK

Lakeside Parkway

ROCKLEDGE PARK

17

Lake Grapevine

N

Veer left when the trail reaches another fork, following the paved road until it becomes a dirt path. Keep left at the next two forks, following the trail as it becomes a paved road again.

At about 3.0 miles cross the road and follow the trail as it turns back into a dirt path, winding through the forest until it reaches the MADD Picnic Shelter at Murrell Park, the turnaround point for this hike.

Miles and Directions

0.0 Start at the trailhead and head up a small hill to reach the lakeshore. Follow the shoreline to reach a series of cliffs.

1.0 Follow the trail as it crosses a small bridge and bear right when the trail widens

1.2 Come to a scenic overlook; follow the trail as it heads into a clearing.

1.6 Cross over a road and head into a picnic area. Pick up the trail as it heads back into the woods.

2.5 Bear left when the trail reaches another fork, following the paved road until it becomes a dirt path. Keep left at the next two forks, following the trail as it becomes a paved road again.

3.0 Cross the road and follow the trail as it turns back into a dirt path. Wind through the forest for another 0.5 mile to the MADD Picnic Shelter at Murrell Park. Retrace your steps to the trailhead.

6.1 Arrive back at the trailhead.

18 Ray Roberts Lake State Park: Johnson Branch Trail

With well-marked paved trails, plenty of picnic tables, and a great swimming beach for a posthike dip, this loop is well worth the drive.

Distance: 3.5-mile lollipop
Approximate hiking time: 1.5 hours
Difficulty: Easy
Trail surface: Concrete pavement
Best season: Mar through Oct
Other trail users: Cyclists
Canine compatibility: Leashed dogs permitted
Fees and permits: Park entrance fee
Schedule: Park open daily 8:00 a.m. to 10:00 p.m.
Maps: TOPO! Texas CD; park

maps available at the front gate or online at www.tpwd.state.tx.us
Trail contacts: Texas State Parks; (940) 637-2294; www .tpwd.state.tx.us
Special considerations: The park offers free guided nature walks on many Saturdays and occasional fireside chats and speakers at the Oak Point Amphitheater. For the latest schedule check www .tpwd.state.tx.us/newsmedia/ calendar/?calpage=s0138

Finding the trailhead: From Denton take I-35 north to exit 483 and head east on FM 3007 for 7 miles. The park entrance is on the right. Continue straight from the entrance until the road ends at Oak Point parking lot. The trailhead is by the boat ramp and the fish cleaning station. GPS: N33 24.388' / W97 02.900'

The Hike

Lake Ray Roberts supplies water to the cities of Dallas and Denton and is named for longtime congressman Ray Roberts,

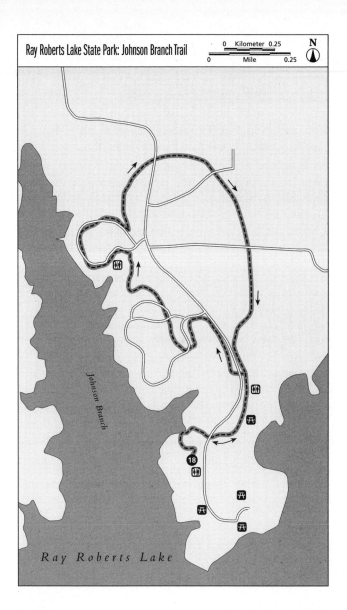

Ray Roberts Lake State Park: Johnson Branch Trail

Johnson Branch

Ray Roberts Lake

18

who died in 1993. The lake encompasses two state parks—Isle du Bois and Johnson Branch—and a collection of protected wetlands and wildlife management areas. The nearby Lake Roberts Greenbelt offers 20 miles of trails, but this park tends to have fewer hikers, making it feel worlds away from the Metroplex even though it makes an easy day trip.

The trailhead is at the back of the park, all the way down the main road, by the boat ramp and fish cleaning station. Look for the concrete-paved trail and bear right, walking away from the parking lot. At about 0.12 mile you'll see the entrance to the Vanishing Prairie Nature Trail. Go left and head into the forested area, which has educational markers identifying trees, plants, and area wildlife. The nature trail is a small loop that eventually returns to the same point.

Rejoin the mail trail and cross the park's main road, heading toward a large swimming area by the lake. The trail follows the shoreline, passing picnic tables on the right. Bear left as the trail splits, crossing back over the park road and heading into the woods and away from the lake. The trail winds through the Juniper Cove camping area here and then meanders back into the woods, passing a chemical toilet on the right.

Cross back over the main park road and head into the woods, looping around until you join the trail back by the beach area. Finish your hike with a refreshing dip in the lake.

Miles and Directions

0.0 Start at the trailhead by the boat ramp and fish-cleaning station adjacent to the parking lot.

0.12 Bear left, following the Vanishing Prairie Nature Trail as it loops by a small pond.

0.4 The nature trail rejoins the main trail. At the main trail bear left and go up small hill, crossing the park road and heading to the beach area.

0.5 At the next trail split, go left, heading into the woods and away from lake.

0.7 The trail crosses back over the main park road.

1.1 Follow the trail through a camping area, bearing left as the trail rejoins the campground road and follows it around loop.

1.5 Cross the main road and go right, heading into the woods as the trail loops around back to the beach.

2.5 Follow the trail as it goes along the lake shoreline, heading back to parking lot and trailhead.

3.5 Arrive back at the trailhead.

19 Fort Worth Nature Center

Hiking with buffalo? The herd here is fenced off, but getting an occasional glimpse of these iconic creatures of the American West adds allure and a photo op to this trail. With more than 3,600 acres of forests, prairies, and wetlands, the Fort Worth Nature Center is one of the largest city-owned nature centers in the United States. Thankfully all that space and the park's entrance fee keep it relatively sparsely populated much of the time. Even on busy weekends, only one or two hikers may be spotted along this trail by the shores of the West Fork of the Trinity River and a forested river bottom.

Distance: 1.8-mile lollipop

Approximate hiking time: 1 hour

Difficulty: Easy

Trail surface: Packed dirt; portions on a wooden boardwalk

Best season: Mar through May; Oct through Nov

Other trail users: Birders

Canine compatibility: Leashed dogs permitted

Fees and permits: Entrance fee; no charge for children under age 2

Schedule: Nature center open 8:00 a.m. to 5:00 p.m. Oct through Apr; 8:00 a.m. to 7:00 p.m. Mon through Fri and 7:00 a.m. to 7:00 p.m. Sat and Sun May through Oct; closed Thanksgiving and Christmas

Maps: TOPO! Texas CD; maps available online at www.fwnaturecenter.org

Trail contacts: Fort Worth Nature Center; (817) 392-7410; www.fwnaturecenter.org

Special considerations: Facilities are limited here, so bring your own food and water. Bring a pair of binoculars and a camera for wildlife viewing and photos.

In addition: Don't miss the prairie dog town, where hundreds of these once-ubiquitous creatures roam their native habitat.

Finding the trailhead: From Loop I-820, exit at TX 199 (Jacksboro Highway) and go west 4 miles. Exit Confederate Park Road to the right and stay on the service road. At the stop sign turn right into the nature center entrance. Stop by the gatehouse to pay the entrance fee and obtain a day pass and a trail map. Follow Shoreline Drive all the way to the end. The trailhead is by the parking lot. GPS: N32 59.955' / W97 29.395'

The Hike

The Fort Worth Nature Center combines three major ecosystems—the Fort Worth or Grand Prairie, the Western Cross Timbers, and the wetlands along the West Fork of the Trinity River. The park's most famous residents, celebrated each spring with the annual Buffalo Boogie race, are its herd of bison, easily viewable from several spots along the park's main drive—the aptly named Buffalo Road. The park's Hardwicke Interpretive Center contains educational exhibits on the park's ecosystems and provides the park's only bathrooms. It's open 9:00 a.m. to 4:30 p.m. Monday through Saturday and noon to 4:30 p.m. on Sunday. Portable toilets are placed around major parking areas, but water fountains aren't, so be sure to pack plenty of liquids before heading out.

Free trail maps are available at the main entrance gatehouse. It's worth pulling over to peruse the varied choices among the center's more than 20 miles of trails. The Canyon Ridge Trail, the most challenging, connects a series of ridges in an up-and-down 3.25-mile trek. The 1.5-mile Greer Island Trail travels over a narrow levee to the small island in the middle of Lake Worth, and the 1.13-mile Prairie Trail leads to the park's prairie dog town.

The hike described here combines three of the park's trails—the Marsh Boardwalk, Riverbottom, and Forked

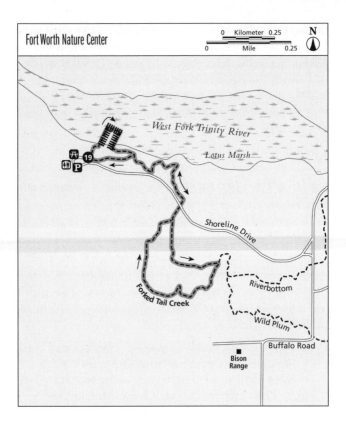

Tail Creek Trails—for a 1.8-mile trek. From the parking lot at the end of Shoreline Drive, the trailhead is by a picnic table and two portable toilets.

Look for the path leading to the Trinity River and down to a boardwalk. Here the trail goes over a large marsh and, depending on water levels, it's possible to view animal tracks on the sandy shoreline. The boardwalk loops over the water and provides a great viewing spot for birds, including the occasional hawk. Where the boardwalk meets the shore, veer left onto the Shoreline Trail and continue along the river as the trail winds alongside Shoreline Drive. When the trail crosses the road, stay straight and enter the woods.

The trail splits just inside the forest. Bear right to get on Forked Tail Creek Trail as it moves deeper into the woods and the path becomes a boardwalk above the mucky soil. The trail surface alternates between packed dirt and boardwalk, and a small stream joins up with the trail. This part of the trail is not as well marked, so be careful to look for signs to make sure you haven't wandered off-trail.

The Forked Tail Creek Trail eventually loops back to join the Riverbottom Trail. Turn left at this junction. The trail makes a right-angle turn and returns to the intersection with Shoreline Drive, where you can return along with river—this time on the right side—back to the parking lot.

Miles and Directions

0.0 Start at the trailhead by the picnic table and head down to the river. Veer left onto the boardwalk, being careful to watch for tall reeds that push through the wooden boards.

0.24 As the boardwalk connects back to shore, bear left onto the Riverbottom Trail, with the river on your left.

0.5 The trail crosses Shoreline Drive and then goes left at a junction, heading into the forest.

0.6 Turn right onto the Forked Tail Creek Trail (look for sign).

1.2 Trail reconnects with Riverbottom Trail. Take a left and cross back over Shoreline Drive, heading back towards the lake.

1.7 Stay straight at the junction with the marsh boardwalk. Take a left and head uphill to the parking lot with the river on your right.

1.8 Arrive back at the trailhead.

About the Author

Kathryn Hopper is a freelance writer and photographer who specializes in outdoor and family-friendly travel in the Southwest. Her other books include *Family Fun Vacation Guide Southwest* and *Fort Worth: Where the Best Begins.* Kathryn loves to explore trails throughout Texas with her husband, Stuart, and their four sons: James, Henry, Will, and Andrew. She lives in Southlake, Texas.

WHAT'S SO SPECIAL ABOUT UNSPOILED, NATURAL PLACES?

Beauty Solitude Wildness Freedom Quiet Adventure
Serenity Inspiration Wonder Excitement
Relaxation Challenge

There's a lot to love about our treasured public lands, and the reasons are different for each of us. Whatever your reasons are, the national **Leave No Trace** education program will help you discover special outdoor places, enjoy them, and preserve them—today and for those who follow. By practicing and passing along these simple principles, you can help protect the special places you love from being loved to death.

THE PRINCIPLES OF LEAVE NO TRACE

- Plan ahead and prepare
- Travel and camp on durable surfaces
- Dispose of waste properly
- Leave what you find
- Minimize campfire impacts
- Respect wildlife
- Be considerate of other visitors

Leave No Trace is a national nonprofit organization dedicated to teaching responsible outdoor recreation skills and ethics to everyone who enjoys spending time outdoors.

To learn more or to become a member, please visit us at www.LNT.org or call (800) 332-4100.

Leave No Trace, P.O. Box 997, Boulder, CO 80306

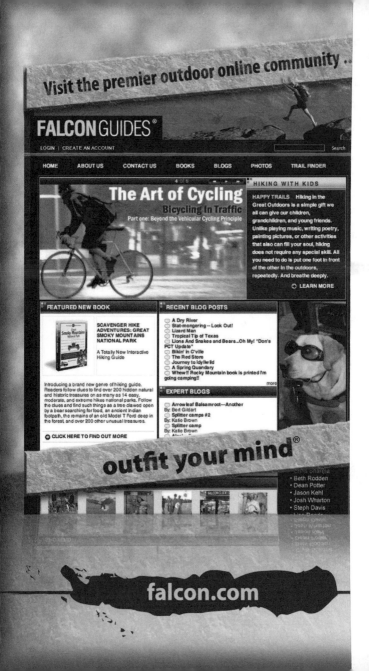